LIVING IN... RUSSIA

by Jesse Burton
illustrated by Tom Woolley

READY-TO-READ

SIMON SPOTLIGHT

An imprint of Simon & Schuster Children's Publishing Division • 1230 Avenue of the Americas, New York, New York 10020
This Simon Spotlight edition May 2018 • Text copyright © 2018 by Simon & Schuster, Inc.
Illustrations copyright © 2018 by Tom Woolley
SIMON SPOTLIGHT, READY-TO-READ, and colophon are registered trademarks of Simon & Schuster, Inc.
For information about special discounts for bulk purchases,
please contact Simon & Schuster Special Sales at 1-866-506-1949 or business@simonandschuster.com.
Manufactured in the United States of America 0318 LAK • 2 4 6 8 10 9 7 5 3 1 • Library of Congress Cataloging-in-Publication Data
Names: Burton, Jesse, author. | Woolley, Tom, 1981- illustrator. Title: Russia / by Jesse Burton ; illustrated by Tom Woolley.
Description: New York : Simon Spotlight, 2018. | Series: Living in . . . series Identifiers: LCCN 2017061246 (print)
LCCN 2018002925 (ebook) | ISBN 9781534417670 (e-book) | ISBN 9781534417663 (hardback) | ISBN 9781534417656 (paperback)
Subjects: LCSH: Russia (Federation)—History—Juvenile literature. | BISAC: JUVENILE NONFICTION / Readers / Beginner.
JUVENILE NONFICTION / People & Places / Europe. | JUVENILE NONFICTION / History / Europe. Classification: LCC DK510.76 (ebook)
LCC DK510.76 .B87 2018 (print) | DDC 947—dc23 LC record available at https://lccn.loc.gov/2017061246

GLOSSARY

Abstract art: a style of art emphasizing the relationship of shapes, colors, and feelings instead of recognizable objects

Barre: a handrail that is attached to the wall; it gives support and balance to people who are exercising.

Ecosystem: the plants and animals that are found in a particular location

Federation: a political organization formed when smaller political groups unite

Fortress: a place that is protected against attack due to parts of its structure, like walls and trenches

Kremlin: a wooden fortress built in the fourteenth century. Its buildings were later made of stone, and now they are made of bricks and modern building materials.

Time zone: a region that shares the same standard of time, based on the Earth's rotation and the path of the sun. There are currently thirty-nine time zones used around the world.

Trans-Siberian Railway: a railway that connects the European section of Russia with its Far East section by crossing the country's Siberian region

Tzar: the title given to a male ruler in Russia; sometimes spelled "csar," "czar," and "tsar"

University: a school that offers courses that lead to a degree

NOTE TO READERS: Some of these words may have more than one definition. The definitions above are how these words are used in this book.

Zdravstvuyte! (say: ZDRAHST-voo-tyeh) That is how we say hello in Russia. My name is Katia. I live in Russia, a country in both Europe and Asia, where more than one hundred forty million people live . . . including me!

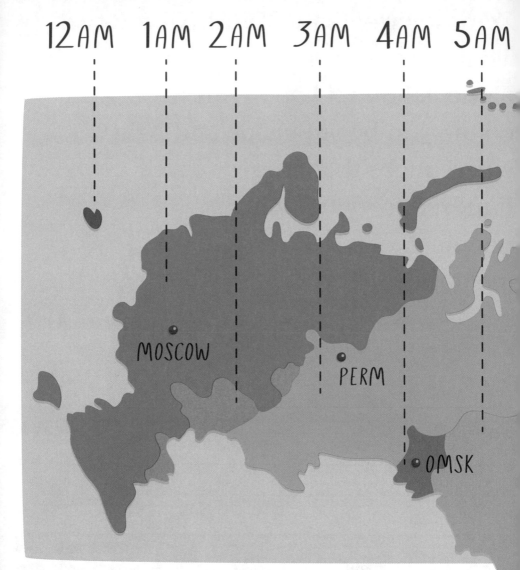

12AM 1AM 2AM 3AM 4AM 5AM

MOSCOW

PERM

OMSK

Russia is the largest country in the world. It takes up almost one-eighth of all the land on the planet. It has coasts on three oceans—the Atlantic Ocean, the Pacific Ocean, and the Arctic Ocean.

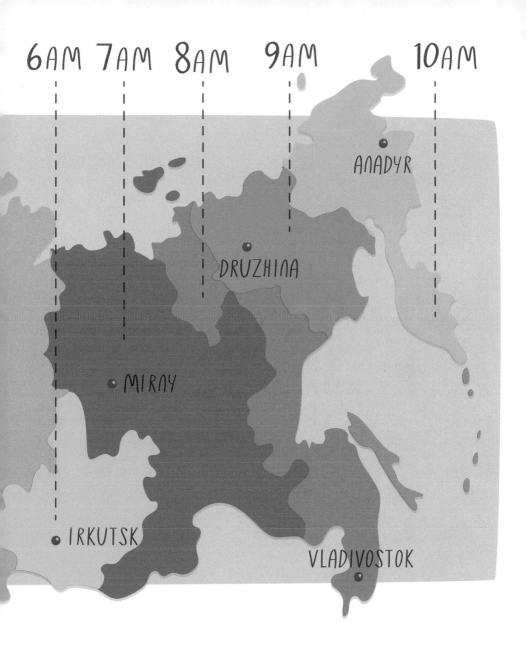

There are eleven time zones in Russia! That means when it is midnight in the western part of Russia, it is ten a.m. on Russia's east coast.

The Russian plain extends from Russia's western border to the Ural Mountains.

To its south is the Caucasus mountain range. At 18,510 feet, Mount Elbrus is the highest peak in the Caucasus range—and in all of Europe!

Siberia is the largest region in Russia. It spans from the Ural Mountains to the Pacific Ocean.

ARCTIC
OCEAN

PACIFIC
OCEAN

Siberia makes up more than three quarters of all the land in Russia, yet only 27 percent of Russia's population lives there. Still, there are plenty of other things living in Siberia!

There are three ecosystems in Siberia. The tundra is in the northern region. Small shrubs and moss grow in the tundra. It is very cold and windy, which is perfect for arctic foxes and snowy owls.

The taiga (say: TIE-guh) region is known for its lush forests. Brown bears and gray wolves thrive in this region.

To the south is the steppe region. Many different animals live on its grassy plains.

Moscow is the capital and biggest city in Russia. The Kremlin is in the center of the city. It used to be a fortress. Government offices, museums, and churches can be found there.

The city of St. Petersburg is located on the Baltic Sea. There are beautiful buildings and museums.

Nizhny Novgorod (say: NISH-nee NOHV-gah-red) is a city located at the intersection of two large rivers. It is a popular hub for business.

Novosibirsk (say: NO-va-sah-BEERSK) is a city in Siberia. Many people, like my family, visit its famous zoo.

Last summer my family traveled more than two thousand miles on the Trans-Siberian Railway from our home in Moscow to Novosibirsk. It took two days.

In Novosibirsk we spent a lot of time at the zoo. There are more than eleven thousand animals there. My mom is a zoologist. She gave a talk at the zoo about Siberian tigers.

Back home, I live in an apartment with my mom, dad, and older brother, Alexander. Our apartment is near the university where my mother teaches.

My father works for an oil company.
He coordinates how oil is transported
and delivered. My brother loves
soccer. He practices any chance he
can—even before school!

In the morning Alexander wakes me up when he gets in from practice. I put on my school uniform and get ready for school. Then I help make breakfast.

Today we eat hot cereal called kasha and drink tea. After breakfast Alexander and I walk to school together. I meet my best friend, Maria, along the way.

School starts at nine o'clock. There are thirty students in my class. We study reading, writing, math, history, science, gym, singing, and drawing.

This morning we are learning about Peter the Great, a famous Russian ruler who united all of Russia. Would you like to hear about him?

In 1672 Peter was born in Moscow. His family was very wealthy, and his father was the tzar (say: ZAR).

When Peter was four, his father died. Peter's brother Ivan became the tzar. Peter was given the title of "Second Tzar," but he did not govern. Instead he studied subjects that interested him, like military operations, navigation, carpentry, and printing.

He met many different people outside of Russia during this time. In 1696 Ivan died, and Peter became the sole tzar. Peter spent the next year touring the great cities of Europe.

When he returned to Russia, Peter began to make changes. He applied what he had learned abroad. He organized Russia's military, established the first Russian newspaper, and looked for better access to trade with Europe. It took more than twenty years, but Russia finally succeeded. They claimed land on the Baltic Sea and built the port city of St. Petersburg.

Peter did not stop there. He stressed the need for math and science in schools. And he sent troops to the farthest part of Russia—all the

way to the Pacific Ocean. In 1721 he formed the Russian Empire.

After history we study math, reading, and writing. Then it is time for lunch. We eat dumplings stuffed with meat and onions called pelmeni (say: pel-MEN-ee) and some fruit. It is very yummy!

When lunch is done, we have science
and then art. Art is my favorite class!
We are learning about abstract art
and how artists use colors and shapes
to show feelings. Today I am feeling
orange and squiggly.

When school lets out at three o'clock, I go to ballet class with Maria. We both love to dance! First we warm up at the barre (say: BAR). We also practice different positions with our feet. This helps us become strong and graceful dancers.

When I get home, it is time
for dinner. We have soup
and roasted chicken with
noodles. We drink
tea sweetened
with jam. Aftcr
dinner my mother
and I get dressed
up for a special
night out.

We are going to see the Bolshoi (say: BOWL-shoy) Ballet! It is one of the oldest ballet companies in the world. Tonight they are performing *The Firebird*. It is based on a Russian fairy tale.

The dancers leap across the stage. Their arms flutter just like bird wings. Maybe I will dance on this stage someday!

I get ready for bed when we return home. I look at the program from tonight's ballet. It shows many interesting places where the ballet dancers perform. They travel all over the world.

My parents tuck me in. I tell them that I would like to travel all over the world and dance when I grow up. Would you like to travel to Russia someday?

ALL ABOUT
Russia

name: The Russian Federation (or Russia for short!)

Population: 144 million

Capital: Moscow

Language: Russian is the official language, but many people speak other languages. Russian is written using the Cyrillic alphabet.

Total Area: 6,601,668 square miles

Government: federation

Currency: ruble

Fun Fact: Peter the Great introduced a tax on facial hair and even shaved off beards at a party thrown in his honor!

Flag: Consists of three equal horizontal bands—white on the top, blue in the middle, and red on the bottom. While there is no official symbolism given to this flag, some believe that white represents generosity, blue represents loyalty, and red represents courage.